THE PSYCHOIC REVOLUTION
Magnify your intuition for more success and a lot less stress

Dr. Stephen Simpson

Copyright © 2018 Dr. Stephen Simpson
All rights reserved.

ISBN: **1717097065**
ISBN-13: **978-1717097064**

DEDICATION

I truly appreciate the fresh thought and support gifted to me by my family Caroline, Lucy, and Ben. They ignited my luck magnet and then the book wrote itself.

Table of Contents

DEDICATION ii
ACKNOWLEDGMENTS v
1 INTRODUCTION 1
2 LESSONS FROM HISTORY 7
3 SNAKES AND LADDERS 15
4 BACK TO THE SWAMP 19
5 NO FEAR 24
6 THE POWER OF THE PINEAL GLAND 29
7 THE POWER OF THE THIRD EYE 32
8 THE POWER OF SPIRITUALITY 37
9 THE POWER OF SYNCHRONICITY 43
10 THE POWER OF THE COLLECTIVE UNCONSCIOUS 48
11 THE POWER OF INTUITION 57
12 CONCLUSION 62
ABOUT THE AUTHOR 69

ACKNOWLEDGMENTS

Sarah Matthew, Tony Wrighton and my agent Robyn Bourne volunteered to read my manuscript too, and I bit off their hands. Their wise and profound contributions are equally appreciated.

I have been hugely influenced by the work of many other opinion leaders without whose contributions our world would look very different today. The ones that I have trained with in person in alphabetical order include Richard Bandler, Paul McKenna, Michael Neill, and Eric Pearl. One of Paul's books did change my life, and little did I know then that he would also become such a valued friend.

1 INTRODUCTION

Thank you for buying this book. If you are reading it for free that is OK with me too. Thanks anyway. My promise to you, whether you paid for the book or not, is that I am going to give my 100% effort to make you lucky. Not a bit lucky, but a lot lucky. This will not happen unless we both get way out of our comfort zone. It will take magic.

Today is December 27, 2017 and we're limping slowly towards the end of the year. For many people, this is the twilight period between the frantic activities of Christmas and the New Year, another excuse for a celebration, which is lurking just around the corner.

The Christmas parties are now over, the presents have been given and received, and many of us would have eaten too much, drunk too much, and not slept enough.

For some it has been a stressful period. Not enough money, too many relatives in too small a space, and no time to call our own. Some people will have fallen sick, some will have injured themselves in car accidents or fights. Some will have fallen in love. Some will have died, some will have been born. It is the whole arc of human experience compressed into just a few short days.

Surely not another book?

Why have I decided to write another book? I have broken my main resolution this year. My willpower cracked with only a few days left to survive, and I have started a new book. Something I said I would never ever do again.

Bizarre as it might sound I did not feel as if the decision was mine. The idea of the book developed a life of its own, and the first draft was completed in less than a month.

This book is going to be very different from my previous ones and will be a journey of discovery for both of us.

My clients do the hard work

My clients have been very different too, and some have been hugely successful in many different ways. I want to know why they have been so successful, so that others, and me, may enjoy more success in our lives too. I will share with you two of these examples of unexpected success now. I do not understand how they happened, but I know they are hugely significant.

One concerns my first client in my current career as a performance coach. She wanted help with her golf. She got it, but I have no idea where this help came from. Three holes-in-one in just three months, and three more since. What would have happened to my new career if my first client, not this one in particular, but whoever it might have been, had not been helped, but had been driven to depression or worse?

I would almost certainly have quit. In case this sounds too fanciful you might be surprised to know that I occasionally receive emails from golfers who have been driven close to suicide by this pernicious game.

Fortunately for me, and for my client, the Invisible Giants were on my side, and within months I was working with top golfers on the European Tour. I guess I got lucky!

The luck continues

My lucky streak did not finish there. Poker is a card game I previously knew little about but am learning more every day. I do understand numbers, and I also know a bit about how our minds work.

Coaching poker players is fun but forms only a small part of my business. I have only worked with a handful of top poker players, but they have all achieved stunning results. What did I do to help them? Again, I do not know, but I have a few ideas, and I am sure to share them with you throughout this book. Because if these players can exceed their expectations, then perhaps you can too. How about that for a thought?

What were the results of my work with these poker players? In terms of numbers, the four players I mentioned earlier earned collectively $413,000 6 months before working with me, and $3,488,000 6 months after working with me.

Those are big numbers by any definition, and me, their coach, not being able to explain where this transformation came from requires further exploration. This is why I feel compelled to attempt to explain the unexplainable, and why this will be my seventh book.

What were the other books about?

The previous books have all been about how we can explore and use the power of our unconscious mind in different ways. They have been practical. Two of the books have been about golf, one of the books has been about sport, two have been about personal development, one is about luck, and the last one was about my work with professional poker players.

These books have all been largely well received by readers and attracted mainly 5-star reviews. They all helped at least some people, as they struggled with their challenges, as I know from the emails I receive. As I finished each book I vowed that it would be my last one. On every occasion, including now, I broke my resolution. So why will this one be different?

This book will be different because:
The book will be not written in a state of fear. It will not ask questions like, what if nobody likes this? What if I am ridiculed for my ideas? What if I cannot prove some of the controversial statements I make? It is important that there will be no fear, because fear causes us to fight, to run away, or just to freeze. None of these options will help any author.

The problem is that these are the kind of questions, and there are many others like them, that surfaced whilst writing my other books. As a result, these books became to some extent books of ideas and quotes from other people, albeit packaged in a way that would hopefully resonate with the reader and ignite new ideas for them to explore.

If in doubt go with the truth

I will do my best to make sure that this book is about truth, the whole truth, and nothing but the truth. The problem of course is that nobody knows what the truth is, so the best I can say is that this book will explore what I truly believe to be the magic ingredients that ignite success.

I will start where I mean to go on and state that I am writing this book partly for selfish reasons. I am writing it because I know that to a certain degree my previous books finished where they should have started. They were books about success and raising our game and they worked for many people, including myself. They provided me with material to use in my coaching programs, to use in my talks, and to use in making my videos. They also made me some money, but the most important thing is that they made me think, and I am still thinking.

Much of my work now is based around the enduring concept of luck, and why I believe that luck is not random. I am not alone. Emperor Napoleon Bonaparte only appointed his generals from the small pool of officers he considered lucky. Tennis champion Roger Federer knows that when he is facing defeat he needs a miracle. He needs to find a way to put luck on his side.

I wrote and talked about luck from a predominantly research and analytical background. In my book *Get Lucky Now* I talk about the seven secrets of successful people. I explained that I can guarantee that almost everybody can attract at least a little more luck into their life if they read this book. The reason I can say this with some confidence is that six of the seven secrets that I wrote about are based on logic and are well proven throughout history.

It is only in the final chapter that I start to feel a little braver. I start to write in more detail about some of the results that my clients have enjoyed. The ones that defy logical explanation or conventional arithmetical analysis. I did not know what to call this chapter, and after much thought settled on one word. Magic.

Time to be brave

I gave a few hints of where magic might come from, and how we might be able to use it ourselves, but I left most, if not all, of these questions unanswered. Looking back, I think I did this for two reasons. First because I did not know the answers, and secondly because I did not wish to be considered either a lunatic or a fraud.

So as a result, the book was written to some extent to appeal to as many people as possible, and as a result drifted away from the magic that was almost certainly the most important part of it.

This book, my last one (?), is my chance to put the record straight, and say what I really think, but in humility, recognising that my beliefs are just that. Firmly held convictions, but still only personal thoughts.

I mentioned earlier that this book would be for me as well as you, and it will be, because writing is the doing part of thinking. Writing this book will make me think, and some of these thoughts are likely to be painful. These just might be the thoughts that will be the most important for both of us.

This book is also different because, unusually for me, I have no plan. I have no idea how many chapters there will be. I do not even know what the title will be yet. There are no mind maps, nor are there any pages of scribbled thoughts to guide me. There is nothing apart from my laptop and a microphone. I'm not even typing. I'm just dictating into a tiny microphone trying to imagine that I'm talking with you right now over a cup of coffee.

I mentioned the first draft was completed in less than a month. It will take much longer to add structure to my thoughts, and for the book to be ready for publication.

No resolutions this year

I mentioned at the beginning of this introduction that we are limping towards the New Year. In previous years, I would have been very excited by this. I would have been looking at last year's plans and marking my performance. What went well? What were my failures? What will my goals be for 2018?

This year I feel very different. I have already told you I broke one of last year's resolutions, the one about not writing another book. There are no resolutions for next year. Because if I have learnt one thing it is that the best things that have ever happened to me were never on a plan. Or at least not on my plan.

I have learnt the hard way that the enemy of the best is the good. Settle for being good, and you will be unlikely to become excellent.

I find this exciting, but it is a different type of excitement. It is an excitement that leaves all options open. If only one of these formless options takes shape it could easily be the best thing that has ever happened to me and reward me a great year.

But of course, the problem is that none of us really knows what a great year is, or even what constitutes a bad year for that matter. So, if you are confused then all I can say is that I am too. But I do have an overwhelming feeling that there will be something valuable in this book for both of us. It will not come from me, it will come from magic.

In the next chapter I will examine our murky past and discuss one of our biggest mistakes. One that we all continue to pay a heavy price for, but one which is fortunately reversible. Keep reading, because you will not win if you do not put yourself in the game!

2 LESSONS FROM HISTORY

Why people write books
If you plan to write a book I do not recommend it. It is quite stressful, the hours are long, and the pay for most authors is low. Despite this there is also a lot of pleasure. Our default state is to be creative and curious, and writing is one form of creation. It can become an obsessive pleasure, as can all forms of creativity, not least because as soon as a book is written, it no longer accurately reflects your current thinking. Which is why new books are written, new sculptures are crafted, and new music composed.

If this has not put you off find somewhere nice to write because it will help your creative juices to flow. I am in Australia because it is snowing in London at the moment, and frozen brains do not work well. I can sit on the balcony surrounded by trees and tropical birds and the days pass very pleasantly. However, life being what it is there is always going to be at least one insensitive soul who spoils my day by asking how many words I have written. At least I have now come up with a title for the book.

Several people have asked me to explain the title *The Psychoic Revolution*. To the best of my knowledge the word psychoic did not previously exist, although I am well aware that nothing is ever unique. So, apologies to anybody else who might have used this word before I did.

I chose this word because I believe it to be "the sweet spot of peak performance that makes people lucky and lives somewhere between the psychotic and psychic state of mind".

I have a strong gut feeling that this sweet spot will have a lot to do with how lucky we can get. I will explain exactly what these words mean later in the chapter, but first the history lesson. I will keep it short and hopefully sweet.

These are our roots

People like you and me have been shambling around this planet for about 10 million years and looked very different then to how we look now. 10 million years in evolutionary terms is just a blink of the eye, and yet we were fast learners. During that time, we have learned how to walk on two legs, use stone tools, make fires, cook food, and eliminate most of our competition, including our close relatives, the Neanderthals.

The Neanderthals disappeared about 30,000 years ago, soon after the humans did something very stupid, and we are now paying a very high price for their stupidity. The extinction of the Neanderthals at this time and our stupid mistake may not be a coincidence.

Our stupid mistake was that we learned how to talk. For over 9 million years we had managed very well without talk. Strangely enough we apparently communicated very effectively. It was much easier then because we lived in very small social groups, probably only one or a few families living together.

We soon learned to interpret the meaning of different grunting sounds, and we certainly understood the ear twisting and hair pulling that often went with the grunts. Occasionally we would bump into a stranger on the forest trail who would not understand our grunts. So, we would kill him before he killed us. Men generally kill more people than women.

During our history before speech we survived every threat that nature put in our way. In other words, we were lucky.

Our big mistake

The reason why learning to talk was such a big mistake is that when we learn a new skill we usually lose an old one that we had previously relied upon. A modern example would be GPS. It is a wonderful invention that allows us to navigate the world to an accuracy of centimetres. As long as it keeps working. When it fails we are lost in more ways than one, because we have lost our innate power of knowing where we are, and how to get to where we want to go.

The skill we largely lost when we learned to talk was that of non-verbal communication. We were experts at interpreting body language, reading emotions, and pattern recognition. We knew many things intuitively, and we acted on our instincts. In other words, we were psychic, or something close to it.

According to the Oxford English Dictionary part of the definition of a psychic is a person who "appears to have powers of telepathy."

The problem we made for ourselves when we learnt to talk is that language is ambiguous, and that words are only an approximation of our thoughts. Our attention span was already starting to become shorter, and through the years it would continue to shorten, and is probably now shorter than ever before in history.

As a result, our conversations would also need to be much shorter. Because our thoughts are so abstract we struggle to find the right words to describe them. Therefore, these thoughts necessarily became generalised, with much content deleted. What is left is distorted by our own personal bias, with the result that very little truth remains. No wonder we get so confused!

These natural distortions make it almost impossible for us to separate fact from fiction. We have lost our psychic abilities and are now developing psychotic tendencies.

According to the Oxford English Dictionary "Psychosis is a severe mental disorder in which thought and emotions are so impaired that contact is lost with external reality."

I certainly do not wish to trivialise a serious and very distressing mental health condition, but I just wonder how much this definition applies to all of us? Psychosis is a spectrum, and my conclusion is that we all suffer mildly from a permanent and probably incurable loss of contact with reality.

As a result of these delusions we have lost the ability to recognise our intuition, which is our psychic power, and as I mentioned a moment ago, the source of luck.

Social media is born

When we learnt to talk we recognised that another person does have some value to us. It might not be very much, but sometimes a little can go a long way. We also learnt a bit about social etiquette by trying out different approaches.

One of the first things that we discovered was not to ask direct questions like, "Where is the nearest bee hive with the sweetest honey?" We soon learnt that a better approach is to say something like this.

"Good morning Sir. How nice to see you and I hope your day is going well? Is there anything I can help you with at the moment? Please excuse me, I just had another thought. I don't suppose by any chance you have found a honeypot on your travels, have you? Oh, thank you so much. It has been a pleasure meeting you, and I hope we meet again soon. Have a nice day."

The talking experiments did not end here. Sooner or later somebody found that it is not the words that one uses that are important, but the way that they are used. This could be the subject of our whole book, or even a library of books. But in summary it is the secret of hypnosis. We are all hypnotists to a greater or lesser extent, and some people are incredibly gifted in this area.

The best hypnotists are often given fancy titles like 'persuasion and influence experts', or 'communication specialists'. They would not see it this way, but very often they tell lies. And much of our success as a species is due to our outstanding ability to lie to each other. Why on earth is this skill so important to our success?

How to build a house

Before we could speak life was a lot simpler. It was 'the good old days' as those who embrace nostalgia might say. We did not do much thinking, and the danger of overthinking is a familiar topic in my chats with people.

Mr and Mrs Caveman knew when they were hungry and so went out to gather some berries or kill and eat whatever was unlucky enough to cross their path. When they were cold they built a fire to keep warm. Tasks like this took up most of the day, and so with nothing to talk about there was not much to think about.

When we did learn to talk to each other we found a way of encoding our formless thoughts into something consciously tangible. We also found from our early conversations that other people sometimes have something that we wanted.

This is an imaginary conversation taken from history soon after we learned to talk, about 50,000 years ago. Richard was one of history's first leaders. This is his story.

"Bob was good at building stuff. We did not like him very much because he had some nasty habits, but we made allowances for it. Bob was also not very generous and turned down our first request for him to build us a nice house like he has, only a bit bigger.

We were tempted to kill him, but fortunately we saw the big picture and came up with a cunning plan. If Bob built our house we would treat his tropical leg ulcers. We felt it better not to share with him the truth that we did not have a clue where to start with his ulcers. We just made some mud, smeared it on his leg, told him it would take some time for them to heal, and he just had to be patient. We also said that exercise would be good for him, particularly climbing up-and-down ladders building houses.

Because we used our best hypnotic voice Bob reluctantly agreed and a few weeks later the house was built. It was not exactly what we planned, but it was good enough. It has never been easy to find a good builder.

Me and my growing family felt quite smug as we sat on our veranda drinking our fortified honey. We felt overall that our experiment with Bob had worked quite nicely.

Unfortunately, Bob was not the easiest person to work with, and a bit of a moaner. He was still banging on about his ulcers. He did not like my explanation that the recovery was slower than anticipated because he was a negative thinker and a bad person. I reassured him in my best hypnotic voice he just needed to focus on cleaning up his aura and being a better person, and his ulcers would surely heal.

Overall, we recognised that whilst you can't please everybody all the time, the experiment had been so successful that it was certainly worth trying out on a few other people. To cut a long story short within the space of two years we had made our own tribe of exactly 150 people. They all had valuable skills to offer the tribe, which was why they were still alive. I was the president because I was the best qualified and the oldest in my family. My family held all the lesser Government jobs.

When something sounds too good to be true I soon learnt to my cost it usually is. Just when things with our tribe were going so nicely we had an outbreak of 'trouble at mill'.

Apparently, a few youngsters had got together and decided that they could do a better job than me. Can you believe it? My tolerance is legendary, but I have to say that I found their behaviour unacceptable. I will spare the gruesome details, but let's just say that sometimes one has to be firm but fair, not forgetting that one of the secrets of influence is to punish traitors without mercy to scare the living daylights out of everybody else.

However, I no longer rested so easily in my bed, because I had an uncomfortable feeling that whilst I might have dealt with this small rebellion it would probably not be the last one. I needed to come up with another cunning plan."

Bad news travels faster than good news

Our ancestor Richard was lucky, because one of the members of his tribe, Ian, knew that most people talk about the same things, usually the topics that cause them pain. So, Ian's advice to Richard was to "Find where the pain is."

Now that the tribe have learned how to speak to each other, they talk a lot of nonsense, and almost all of it is untrue. It does not necessarily mean they are lying, they are just deluded, a little psychotic.

This is what Ian said,

"Find out what they are worrying about, give them a solution to it, and a compelling reason to follow you as their leader for ever. Then they will be happy even though they have to work more hours. More importantly you will also be happy, and a lot richer than before.

As long as there are simple rules for everybody to adopt, and as long as there is a prize for compliance people will usually do what you want them to do. The prize does not even have to exist.

So, everybody is happy, more or less. They know the rain will come and the crops will grow because you said that you would take care of this with your magic. You are the happiest person of all because every else is doing all the work, and you can relax and enjoy your well-earned fortified honey."

As a footnote Bob the Builder is also a bit happier because he has other people to help him and has stopped moaning about his leg ulcers. Richard's family are very happy because they are now living in a palace. This is a story that will be repeated many times right up to the present day, and presumably beyond.

One for the pencil monitor

An observer might point out that the tribe are now working longer hours for less money than before and are not noticeably happier than before. Indeed, in our present-day society people are living longer than ever before, having more babies than ever before, and having more personal possessions than ever before, yet the incidence of stress-related disease is also higher than ever before.

As Ian explained to Richard,

"I guess it has always been like this. The rich get richer and the poor get poorer."

Richard did not allow these criticisms to weaken his cunning plan. Indeed, the plan worked much more successfully than he expected, as he boasted,

"I am now an emperor ruling my empire. My family are helping me because they are the only people I can trust. Although I am starting to have a few doubts about their loyalty and think it could soon be time for another cull."

On the one hand it could be argued that we do not have much to show for our millions of years of evolution. We do not appear to be any more intelligent than Richard and his tribe, and we have less practical skills. Yet on the other hand despite our self-delusions we have never had it so good. We now have the benefit of modern medicine, live longer than ever before, rarely starve for more than a day or two, unless we are on a trendy diet, and yet the rates of some mental illnesses are higher than ever before in history.

Stuck in reverse gear

Because the truth is that none of us knows how to do very much apart from talk and tell lies. Very few people would be able to build their own house, gather their food, or kill an animal to eat. In other words, they would be totally incapable of surviving.

Although people enjoy the illusion of free thought most of these thoughts they value so highly are only hallucinations. We have forgotten how to trust our most important gift, our gut instinct, also known as intuition. But it is never too late. I am hopeful that as this book progresses we can become more psychoic. What do I mean by this?

The psychoic state of mind
I propose that it is possible to keep the benefits that come from the creativity of our mild degree of psychosis, and at the same time regain at least some of our lost psychic powers. As a result, our mental health just might improve.

This gifts us the opportunity to develop the psychoic state of mind, develop our powers of intuition, and get lucky. The psychoic state of mind is the sweet spot of peak performance that makes people lucky, and lives somewhere deep in our reptile brain, somewhere between the psychotic and psychic states of mind.

I hope this history lesson was not too boring. My history lessons at school were dreary to an extreme. It is only now that I recognise the importance of history, because if we understand history we are a lot closer to being psychoic. I also know it was not the history that was boring, but the teachers. I hope times have changed.

In the next chapter I will review how our thinking often stifles our creativity and presents a huge obstacle in our search for success. It prevents us from getting lucky, but fortunately there are some solutions, and they are not too difficult to understand.

3 SNAKES AND LADDERS

Our progress on the path of life is rarely linear. More often it is a series of big leaps forward, usually followed by a crashing fall. We will do well to remember the common expression that pride comes before a fall.

At such times our thinking often stifles our creativity and presents a huge obstacle in our search for success. It prevents us from getting lucky, but fortunately there are some solutions, and they are not too difficult to understand.

Fear of failure

This is probably the first time in my life when I have embarked on a major project without a plan, and so every day is a surprise. In my role as a mind coach many of my clients have a project that they wish to complete, but for one reason or another are stuck.

We are all born to be creative and a life lived without unleashing this talent will not be as fulfilled as it could be. So why do people get stuck? To the best of my knowledge there's one main reason. It is fear. It is the fear of not being good enough, it is the fear of not having enough time, it is the fear of not having enough motivation. There are other reasons but these are the main ones.

There is a solution to these barriers and it is not rocket science. But before I share it with you let us remind ourselves about why we might want to be a bit more psychoic.

We will start with the definition of psychosis, from OED again.

"Psychosis is a severe mental disorder in which thought and emotions are so impaired that contact is lost with external reality."

It can be easy to forget that psychosis is a spectrum. Some people are very psychotic and this can be very serious, but fortunately most of us are much less so. What we all share is a huge problem understanding the difference between reality and fiction.

I mentioned in the last chapter that much of our conversations with each other, and indeed with ourselves, are not based on reality. Most of the time we are unaware of this, and so we are lying to ourselves or to others. This is definitely not a criticism. It is just the way it is.

Unfinished projects

Let me share an example with you. A lot of people want to write a book, but very few people do. Some of those who do write a book do not publish it, usually because they think it is not good enough.

This is rather sad because how many wonderful books, songs, sculptures, and other works of art have not been completed because their creators lied to themselves?

The reason why people get stuck with their projects is because they believe these lies. The truth is they are the last person to judge whether they, or their projects, are good enough. They have also not fully appreciated the joy of creating something, irrespective of whether others like it or not, and how it can be so liberating. The satisfaction of completing a project has little to do with other people, but a lot to do with how we think about ourselves.

We have been brought up to believe in the importance of the big picture, the importance of the plan, and the importance of mobilising massive willpower to complete it. And I have been as guilty as anybody else. It has taken me a long time to recognise the error of my ways, but better late than never.

One of the reasons why plans don't work is that as soon as they have been hatched they are already history. They severely limit our freedom of action, and stifle fresh thought. I have to continually remind myself that our overarching mission is to create more luck for ourselves, and we will do this by using stuff that is useful and ditching the rubbish. We want the fresh thoughts that the psychotic mind can produce, but only those thoughts that are predominantly based on reality.

So where does the psychic fit into this equation? This is an extract from our earlier definition, a psychic is a person who "appears to have powers of telepathy."

If we can reduce the amount of psychotic rubbish in our head and find a way to use the good ideas we will have made a great start. We will have put ourselves firmly in the game. Every word in this book will help us to do this, not because the words are brilliant, but because words force thought. On occasions the links will be very obscure, including to me. These are concepts that are difficult to explain, and I will do my best come up with metaphors that will help us to make these huge mental leaps.

These huge mental leaps will not come from harnessing massive will power, but from our unconscious mind. These leaps will enable us to process a lot more information, and much of this would ordinarily be out of our reach. As a result, our heightened intuition will catapult us to a higher level of sensory awareness than we might think possible. In other words, we will start to look a lot like a psychic. This is the result that the psychoic revolution hopes to achieve.

Frightened of shadows
Back to the creative person who is stuck. As I mentioned earlier they are stuck because of fear. All the other reasons they have highlighted are usually just carefully constructed excuses either to abandon the project before it has started, or to prepare for the inevitability of its failure.

The beauty of having no plan is that it at a stroke eliminates fear. Because if you do not know what the next word is going to be, let alone the next chapter, what is there to fear? Absolutely nothing, and the removal of pressure stimulates those creative juices that can make us get very lucky.

Many of the problems that we are so good at inventing will not actually happen. If they do there is also a very good chance that something else unexpected has also happened, and already taken care of at least some of these problems. And we did not need to do a thing.

There is something else that I should perhaps remind you about, as I mentioned earlier. If you are brave enough to embark on your project without a plan your progress will not be linear. It is far more likely to be a game of snakes and ladders with some good days, and other days where you feel as if you're slithering down a very long snake with a huge ladder left to climb.

I guess that is why they say that patience is a virtue. Experts extol that it is the journey that will provide more fun than reaching the top of the ladder. I certainly hope so!

In the next chapter we will retrace our roots and will be back in the swamp. Because if we can identify where our thoughts come from we will be able to understand ourselves, and others, much better. And it will also help us to become truly psychoic.

4 BACK TO THE SWAMP

I found this chapter difficult to write. Not because of the technical content, nor because of my lack of thoughts. We all have good days, and we all have bad days. On bad days we have no difficulty finding an external reason for our negative emotional state. We might put it down to finding our car had a puncture when we were already late for an appointment. We rarely remind ourselves that on a good day this would only have been a minor inconvenience. We are human beings and it is normal to have a range of emotions on any given day. Usually our internal state of mind determines our mood more than external events, although we are usually the last person to recognise this.

The reason I found this chapter difficult to write was because a trusted reviewer had written me a note saying how much he was enjoying reading the book so far. So far so good. His next words floored me, "because I have no idea what is coming next."

Our doubts are traitors

As soon as I read these words I had an uneasy feeling in my stomach. I did not know where it was coming from, but I knew it was significant. Over the years I have developed and learned to trust my intuition. So why did these words have such a strong effect on me?

Rather than going away the feelings got stronger. I had a restless night, and when I woke up I was in no fit state to continue writing. I was in the mental state that poker players call 'on tilt'. I was full of doubts which were strangling my judgement. It was like having a python wrapped around my neck.

And then an Invisible Giant came to my rescue, and not for the first time either. I suddenly realised why the reviewer's words about having no idea where the book was leading had such a profound effect on me. It was because they were exactly my thoughts too, although I had done my best to block them.

It took longer than it should have done for me to realise that the whole point of this book is just that. In a later chapter I will explain in more detail why keeping plans flexible is a core element of peak performance and getting lucky. Not having a plan is one of the magic ingredients of the creative process. It provides a blank piece of paper. It provides an empty playing field. Which means that absolutely anything is possible. All I have to do is show up for the game and see what happens next.

I had fallen into the same trap that I have spent the first three chapters trying to help others to avoid. So please read these words again and again whenever you find yourself on tilt.

Baby talk

Now I have got this python off my neck I think we are now ready for our new adventure in the swamps. I warn you in advance that you may never think the same way about yourself ever again. You have two choices. You can turn back or you can be brave. Trust me, I am a doctor!

One of the first things I learnt at Medical School was how a healthy human baby develops in the mother's womb. I was introduced to too many very long words and a lot of complicated anatomy. Therefore, I did not enjoy this subject. Apart from one thing.

One of the lecturers explained that as the baby develops it passes through many evolutionary steps, including the development of its brain. At various times of its development the brain resembles a fish brain, then a reptile brain, and at other times a bird brain, until finally, it is a human brain.

In later years as a surgeon I saw at first hand clinical evidence that supported this evolutionary developmental view. Occasionally we would discover that a patient had pouches in their throat. Normally they would be incidental findings on x-rays, but occasionally these pouches would become blocked with food particles and become infected. This condition required urgent surgical intervention. What were these pouches? They were remnants of the gills that fish use to breathe, and there are many similar examples in our body.

Another of these examples is our third eye. It will be a very important part of becoming psychoic, and we'll talk more about this in a later chapter for sure.

Our slimy brain

The reason why I relate these seemingly unconnected anecdotes is to emphasise that when we visit the swamp we will understand a lot more about what we think about, and where these thoughts come from. There is a bit more science stuff to consider first, and I will make it as simple as I can, so take a deep breath.

The brain can be divided into three main areas, and they have links to the evolutionary process that I mentioned.

The outside layer of the brain is called the neocortex. It is the most recent development and only developed about 2 million years ago. This is the part of the brain where we do all our conscious thinking. This is the place where we make pictures and listen to words and analyse information. It is the bit of the brain that makes us intelligent.

The problem is that most of the pictures and words that we invent are not real. They are hallucinations. Yet they are so detailed that we believe they are real. That is why we love to talk about these things to ourselves, and to other people. Many of these artificial constructs are innocent lies. Unfortunately, this is the conscious part of the brain where you and I spend most of our time, surrounded by these slithering untruths.

If we dig a little deeper into the brain we will find what is called the limbic system. This is the home of our emotions, instincts, and beliefs. In contrast to our neocortex this is not such a creative part of our brain. Much of it is hardwired and therefore difficult if not impossible to reprogram. Many of these neurochemical functions are concerned with babies. Making them, feeding them, and protecting them until they eventually become adults. As many parents know this cycle can last 50 years or more. Humans spend more time nurturing their young than any other species, and much of this behaviour is unconsciously programmed.

The limbic system is also where we can find the origins of addictions if we search hard enough. Sigmund Freud enjoyed poking around in this part of the brain. The limbic system is also a relatively recent evolutionary development and has been churning inside our skulls for only about 150 million years.

We are just small dinosaurs

If you are brave enough we can dig a little deeper and it may not come as a total surprise to know that we are now at the reptilian level of the brain, also known as the basal ganglia. This area started to develop in fish about 500 million years ago, and continued its development in amphibians, and reached its final stage in reptiles about 250 million years ago, many millions of years before our ancestors emerged.

Perhaps also not surprisingly the reptilian brain is where our most primitive instincts live. Many of them are directly concerned with our survival and how we respond to threats. It is the home of aggression, of how we protect our territory, and the ritual displays that we use to get our own way. These behaviours go back at least 500 million years.

If we wish to be truly psychoic this model of our brain is going to be very important indeed. It will literally turn your head upside down. It may come as a shock to know that most of the thinking that you are aware of is not actually being created in the most recently developed and intelligent part of your brain. Yet you totally believe that it is.

In reality almost all of your thoughts are arising from the swamp. Of course, they will be filtered and processed by the higher layers of your brain. This sanitation exercise is an essential function to all of us as one of the secrets of our success as a species is that we have evolved as social animals. If people really knew what we were thinking about them we would have few, if any, friends.

Knowing where your thoughts are coming from is a huge advantage that is often not fully recognised. This knowledge will help you to understand why you are sometimes on tilt and help you to find a better place in your brain to move to when necessary.

The experts tell us that we have at least 70,000 thoughts every day. They may well be right but I suspect we have a lot more than this. What is certain is that it is not physically possible to have so many thoughts entering our conscious mind. This is good news because it means that we do have a degree of control over which formless thoughts we allow to take shape and become good ideas. We also know which thoughts to suppress.

The most valuable thoughts are those that rise from the swamp as unpolished diamonds. We probably have millions every day to choose from. The problem is that the harder we try to find these diamond thoughts the less likely we are to find them. I know this is very counterintuitive, but very often in the field of peak performance less is more.

Which is why overthinking, over-planning, and being overcritical will stifle your source of creativity. It does take courage to literally change the habits of a lifetime, but it can be done. I hope the following chapters will help you to find this courage and the techniques to find your magic.

This is enough for the moment. It has not been the easiest chapter to write for many reasons, not least because so many of these ideas require to be felt rather than understood. Don't give up, it will get easier. Trust me. Keep yourself in the game and who knows? You might just score the winning goal!

In the next chapter we will explore the subject of fear in more detail. The reason is simple. Fear is not such a big problem, but the way that many of us think about it certainly is. Think about it in a different way, and there is a good chance you will be a lot happier, carry a lot less stress, and might just be a bit luckier too. If this book only achieves this result in one person it will have been worth writing it.

5 NO FEAR

Quite a lot of the heavy work is behind us and we are almost ready to apply some of this new knowledge to real life situations. Before we can move on though there is one more subject that we must consider, and this subject is fear. More accurately it is about how we choose to think about fear, because I think we all get very confused about fear.

Just as the last chapter was challenging, so too is this one. Like many people just before I go to sleep I review the day. What went well? What did not? What are the lessons to learn for the future? I then spend just a little time planning the next day. Last night was no exception, except that I spent far too long thinking about fear, and what I was going to write.

Why could I not just trust the process and see what the Invisible Giants will have put on my plate overnight? The answer to this question is that I am a human being, and no amount of coaching or thinking is likely to change this. Though whilst I cannot change this, I certainly can change the way I think about it.

So last night I chose to accept lack of sleep as a blessing. It gave me time to think without any other distractions. The conclusion I came to was that I needed some help. It was time to call for the Invisible Giants again. If you are familiar with the work of Napoleon Hill you will know exactly what I mean. If not, do not worry, because I will address this subject in a later chapter.

Eventually I drifted back to sleep, and when I woke up the next morning I knew with a fair amount of certainty how to plot the next leg of our journey. The last chapter prepared us for what is to come now, and hopefully gave us a deeper level of understanding about where our thoughts are hatched.

No fear

I will start with a provocative statement. Fear is not a problem. The problem is the way we think about fear, and this is why many of us are so confused.

I know something about fear, and I know people who know a lot more about fear than I do. I have been exposed to fear on a number of occasions. The first time was during selection for airborne training. I was 18 years old at the time and considering a military career if I did not pass the examinations for medical school. At the time my grades were poor, and this seemed to be a very likely consequence.

The airborne selection process included completing an assault course. I had plenty of previous practice at this without any particular problems and enjoyed it. The problem this time was that the assault course was high up in the trees and we did not have any safety harnesses or nets. If we lost our balance it is likely we would be severely injured or worse. As I climbed step-by-step higher up the trees I had a panoramic view of the forest, most of which I did not want to see. Particularly the lines of military ambulances waiting to cart off the casualties.

Somehow, I got through this ordeal and to this day do not know how. Since then I have spent most of my career in war zones and in challenging locations working as a doctor. I have been under fire, mortar attack, ambush, imprisonment, riots, robbery and probably a few other things too.

I have also had periods of illness including a near death experience with malignant malaria. As if this is not enough, in my medical capacity I have been exposed to countless cases of major trauma arriving in the emergency room.

So why am I sharing this with you? It is not for pleasure because these are painful but fortunately distant memories. I am sharing them with you for one reason. Because I had no fear once I started the assault course, nor did I have any fear during the other experiences. The nearest I came to fear was climbing up the ladder to the top of the trees, and this was not fear, but anxiety.

Once I started the assault course there was no fear. There was something else, and I feel more than a little uncomfortable to say this, but what I felt was difficult to describe but extremely pleasant. I experienced a mental clarity and detachment from normal emotions that was like living in the eye of the hurricane.

We live in worrying times
What this taught me is that the confusion that many of us share is that we mistake anxiety for fear, and I am far from the first person to recognise this. Anxiety is far more common than fear and is definitely not an emotion that we can enjoy. I suspect that we all have periods of anxiety. I certainly do, but far less than I used to. Because I know how to deal with anxiety, now that I know where anxiety comes from. Just this knowing this is like a vaccination and protects me from the insidious effects of anxiety.

At the moment I probably know more about the effects of anxiety than you do. It is not because I am more intelligent than you or more anxious. It is just because I am a doctor and a mind coach, and I see the effects of anxiety every day in my work.

I see at first-hand how anxiety can cause physical illness such as heart disease and even cancer. I see on a daily basis the mental effects of anxiety which include the suffocation of the creative force that would otherwise help us to be successful and attract luck to us as a magnet attracts iron filings. I see on a daily basis how anxiety eats into the dreams and hopes and aspirations of normal people. I see on a daily basis how many wonderful creative projects are abandoned, not because of fear, but because of anxiety.

Fear is not the main cause of abandoned projects because it can be dealt with in the moment, and we have incredibly powerful hormones and neurotransmitters that are primed to help us instantly. These responses are hardwired and do not require any effort on our part to release them. They are always there, ready to be called upon as necessary.

However, anxiety is a very different kind of fish, perhaps I should say reptile. Anxiety is the complete opposite of the in-the-moment experience of fear. Anxiety is a hallucination, and we have already shared our thoughts about how so much of our conscious thinking is based upon fantasy rather than reality.

If you can find a way to think about anxiety in a different light it will be one of the most liberating things you will achieve in your life. Perhaps you have doubts, but I know you can do this, and I promise you that this is a subject that will feature very highly throughout the rest of this book. How you will make this change is a different question, with possibly a different answer. We will have to leave this question unanswered for the moment.

I mentioned that knowing where true fear comes from is a vaccination. Fear lives in a deep part of our brain, almost certainly the reptilian part. It has been around for millions of years for a very good reason. Without it we would not have survived. Men and women have always been exposed to fear and presumably always will. Not surprisingly evolution or creation has taken care of this problem, and the solution lies within us.

Not so with anxiety. Anxiety is a relatively new phenomenon, and it probably only reared its ugly head when we learned how to talk to each other, and tell our stories, and share our fantasies as if they were real. The bottom line is that anxiety is coming from our conscious mind and is a hindrance that we can do well without.

I hope this explains why the last chapter about living in the swamp was a necessary step on our journey. It provides a partial vaccination for dealing with anxiety. Fear not, I have another cocktail to add, but we are not quite ready for it yet.

Small steps and giant leaps

When I started writing this book and putting my ideas together I felt that it was going to have a wide arc, and indeed hinted at this in the introduction. I still believe this to be true. This chapter is probably about as serious as it gets. My plan is that the arc will now lead us into more positive areas. Areas which will empower us to take control of our lives and attract the luck I feel is within touching distance for us both.

This is not a journey where we can jump from A to Z. We have to touch all the other letters in the right order for any of this to make any sense at all. Now we know a bit more about anxiety and where it comes from it should be a little clearer why many people do not achieve success with their projects or abandon them before they started.

The usual culprits that haunt our mind are the hallucinatory beliefs that wear the convincing mantle of reality. The beliefs that our special project or journey through life will not succeed. The beliefs that we do not have all information we require, the necessary skills, the physical and mental energy, the contacts, the will power, the time, or the money.

There are answers to most, if not all, of these self-limiting beliefs. They are not answers that you need to know now. What will be helpful is recognising that many of the identified problems at the beginning of a project are often not problems as the project develops. Because these problems either go away on their own, or a solution appears as if by magic.

I call this the work of the Invisible Giants and we would be lost without it. Solutions appear as if by magic, by coincidences, by lucky interventions, and by synchronicities. Synchronicity is going to be a very important element in concocting our cocktail of luck and will allow us to drink deep from this cup.

In the next chapter I will introduce the tiny organ called the pineal gland. It is a perfect example of less is more, because although it is small it just might be our most important organ. Descartes considered this tiny gland to be the seat of the soul and modern scientists believe it might be the home of joy. Plenty to think about.

6 THE POWER OF THE PINEAL GLAND

Congratulations on making it to this point in the book. We are about halfway through our journey, and it should start to get easier from now. This is a good point at which to mention more details about how people can raise their game to at least the next level.

The first approach is to learn new techniques and add them to your daily routines. This can be helpful but has its limitations. The second approach is just to change the way you think about life, and your place in it. Hopefully this might have happened since you started reading this book. Even just making a decision to buy a book like this can ignite some hidden part of the unconscious mind. The third approach is to do nothing different, other than trust that some unseen force is guiding you and go with the flow. By the time you reach the end of this book these options, and which one is the most likely to help you, will become clearer.

Either way you have a high chance of getting lucky any time from now, and it would not surprise me if your luck was already kicking in. You have put yourself into the game. Once we put a stake in the ground the rest of the fence often starts growing on its own. I learnt that trick in Africa, and it is literally as well as metaphorically true.

I think this next section should be the last bit of brain science, and once again I will do my best to keep it as short and simple as possible. I repeat my previous warning that if you use this material in your neuroscience examination you will fail and will probably be thrown out of the class.

I spent more time thinking on the balcony today, and the birds were fascinated by the two electrodes attached to my forehead. I think you are starting to get a few ideas about what I am getting up to. The reason why I am excited about this chapter is that it provides the stepping point to our third eye. This can be hugely important in attracting success and raising our game to a much higher level than we could have imagined.

Big is good, tiny is better

We owe this to a very small part of our brain called the pineal gland. It is only about the size of a grain of rice, and is shaped like a pine cone, hence its name. It is located deep within the brain and exactly in the midline. It produces an important hormone called melatonin which regulates sleep and synchronises our body clock with time and the seasons. Melatonin is also involved in the production of other hormones, some of which make us happy and even joyful. In my experience happy people are lucky people, and usually successful at whatever they do.

In previous times the pineal gland did not receive very much attention from the scientists and was considered of little practical importance. As an example, years ago as a surgeon I reviewed many routine skull x-rays following head injury and often noticed a collection of tiny white granules in the midline. One day I asked a radiologist what they were. Not important, he said, this is just partial calcification of the pineal gland. Now we know this calcification is linked to dementia and may be a predictor of early aging, so it is very important indeed.

How wrong people can be, even the experts. The first clues that the pineal gland just might be very important came from finding that it possesses a profuse blood supply. Only the much larger kidney has a greater flow. As Chinese medicine instructs us, where the blood flows the energy will follow. As if this was not proof enough of the importance of this tiny gland, it also has a well-developed network of nerves leading to and from it. They are surely there for a reason.

It is not only the scientists that are excited by the pineal gland, and the role it plays in our life. As long ago as the 17th century the philosopher and scientist René Descartes described the pineal gland as "the principal seat of the soul and the place in which all our thoughts our formed." Descartes believed that we consist of a body and soul, and that these are connected by, guess what, the pineal gland.

He was not the only one who was convinced of its importance. The Hindus believe that this gland is the third eye, and one of the seven chakras of the body. There are many other mystical, metaphysical, and occult theories concerned with the role of the pineal gland. As you would guess these are very controversial, and if you require hard science to justify some of these theories you will be very disappointed. Indeed, there is not very much hard science on any subject, just lots of theories that may or may not be true.

If on the other hand, like me, you are prepared to experiment and keep an open mind about these theories the results might just blow your mind. In the nicest possible way of course. I regard the third eye as one of my most important organs. Not only in my work, but in every aspect of my life. The third eye will be the subject of the next chapter, and I will share some ideas about how it developed in the animal kingdom, and how you can make it work for you.

7 THE POWER OF THE THIRD EYE

In the last chapter we talked about the tiny but incredibly powerful pineal gland. I also introduced the concept of its possible direct linkage to the third eye. Like many others I was introduced to the third eye at the age of 17 through the fictional books of the author Lobsang Rampa. The same books were also my first introduction to Tibetan Buddhism, and the concept of astral travelling. These are interests that have fascinated me ever since.

Two eyes are good, three eyes are better
The third eye is without a shadow of doubt another stepping stone along the path of the psychoic revolution. Whether it is real or imaginary does not concern me. All I know is that just being aware of the concept of having a third eye as my friend helps me enormously in my work and can help you too.

The third eye, if it exists, is located between the eyebrows, but a little higher in the area of the forehead. It is sometimes referred to as the mind's eye, and with good reason. In biology it is known as the parietal eye and exists in varying degrees in many animals. Its origin is likely to be primitive because it is most pronounced in the fossils of dinosaurs, where a distinct hole in the skull can be found. Smaller indentations can be found in living amphibians and reptiles, but not in birds and mammals for some reason.

As well as bone indentations the third eye exists physically as nervous cells in most lizards, frogs, and some fish including species of tuna and sharks. It is always covered by a layer of skin, so is not capable of sight in a conventional way. Its cells sense only light, but not images. These sensory inputs are sent to the pineal gland where they help calibrate the circadian rhythm of night, day, and seasons.

In humans there is some evidence the third eye provides its sensory information regarding our position when our eyes are closed. An example would be navigating one's way around a dark room. If you were designing a human being from scratch an argument could be made for having a fully functional third eye in approximately the same position that it exists in animals. Navigators know that three points are needed to fix a position accurately. If we had three eyes our three-dimensional perception would be so much improved.

I have used this tripod concept with professional tour golfers when they have trouble reading the detailed contours of the putting green. On occasions this has been a hilarious experiment but has sometimes been very successful. If something isn't working be prepared to try a different approach, and you just might get a pleasant surprise.

Whilst this information is hopefully interesting, it does not really help us in our search for luck, inspiration, and becoming psychoic. I suggest we continue our search farther afield in the realm of spirituality and mysticism for further clues.

Many Eastern religions embrace the concept of the third eye, and it is sometimes known as the sixth chakra. It is associated with enlightenment, the ability to see chakras and auras, and responsible for out of body experiences. It is also associated with precognition and clairvoyance. If this is so we have stumbled across a true diamond in our search to get lucky. Do you remember the definition of psychic? Let me remind you of its definition lifted from chapter 2. A psychic is a person who "appears to have powers of telepathy."

Can this be explained by simple intuition? I believe it can, and I will come back to this point in a later chapter. I regard intuition in the same way as any other gift. The more you use it, the stronger it becomes. An equally valid statement is, "if you don't use, it you lose it". I will also share more thoughts about this in a later chapter.

Open your eyes

I mentioned earlier that I have always been interested in out of body experiences, and their possible associations with the third eye.

As a hospital doctor I saw several examples of this at first hand, as have many other doctors. When a patient's heart stops beating the nurses send out a crash call. If you are on the resuscitation team you stop whatever you are doing immediately, and sprint to the victim. There are literally only seconds to save a life, and sometimes the patient is lucky. When they regain consciousness, they may describe being drawn to a bright light, and feel a sensation of calm, often with religious overtones.

I have had one out of body experience, but it was not exactly the same as this. Back in 1995 I was working in Nigeria, and to cut a long story short developed a serious form of malaria. By the time it was diagnosed I was in a pretty bad way. I remember when the disease was at its worst crawling to the bathroom with great difficulty.

Before I knew what was happening I found myself looking down at my body with a sense of detached sympathy but knowing that this person's suffering would not last much longer. I thought this person, me, was going to die, and I was not afraid.

The next thing I was aware of was being back in bed several minutes later. I still felt terribly ill but knew then I would survive. The senior nurse visited me at lunchtime and was not convinced. He assessed my condition and told me bluntly I required medical evacuation to Europe for advanced treatment. This would have been hugely costly and difficult to arrange, and I was convinced that it was not necessary.

I persuaded the nurse to give me four more hours, and if my condition had not improved he could go ahead and make the arrangements. Fortunately, my fever broke, and although I still felt desperately ill I knew I was out of danger.

I said this would be an honest book and I have not told many people this story. I relate it now because you will understand why I hold such strong convictions around these controversial concepts. It is not necessary to go anywhere near these lengths to discover how to use the power of your third eye. Whole books have been written on this subject, and I do not claim to be an expert. All I can tell you is what works for me. I use third eye techniques in two main ways. When I work with clients, and at night, when I am wrestling with problems.

My clients come from all backgrounds. The only common factor is that most of them are facing challenges that have been resistant to other forms of therapy or interventions. I suppose I am the last resort, and I'm not quite sure how to think about this! In other words, all of the conventional avenues have been explored, which leaves only unconventional options remaining.

A typical initial consultation with these clients will last about one hour. This is not much time to produce some kind of positive therapeutic response, and in the past, I found this challenge extremely daunting. However, now I approach such consultations in a far more relaxed state. All I have to do is metaphorically switch on my third eye and get out of my own way. Almost always there is a lightbulb moment, and we both sense a way out, and progress has been made. This is not necessarily a third eye experience, but it certainly forms an important part of my therapeutic approach.

Call for the cavalry

The other way I use my third eye is for myself. I use it just before I go to sleep, or if I wake up in the middle of the night. In each scenario my eyes are closed but I imagine I can see through my eyelids. I also try to sense a feeling of fullness in the area of the third eye. Mystics sometimes imagine a whirling disc in this area, which rotates either clockwise or anticlockwise. I have tried this technique but prefer to keep things simple. I will also be guiding my thoughts. I may or may not use a mantra, but I will always ask a question for my unconscious mind to solve while I sleep and dream.

Sooner or later I fall asleep, have dreams, and often the answer to the question surfaces then, or when I wake up. I fancifully refer to it as astral travelling, but it could equally validly be described as just finding another way to communicate with my unconscious mind.

This approach is by no means unique. Similar accounts can be found going back hundreds or even thousands of years. As another example, earlier in this book I referenced Napoleon Hill. He wrote a very popular book called *Think and Grow Rich* and describes a similar approach to find inspiration and answers to problems. So, this is a technique worthy of your consideration at the very least.

There are other methods I use to open the third in either myself or my clients. They include meditation, hypnosis, and by using bioresonance devices. These devices explain why at times I sit on my balcony alone with my thoughts, and with electrodes attached to my forehead.

What all these methods share in common is that they stimulate the particular type of brain waves that are most beneficial when opening gateways to the massive power of the unconscious mind. A detailed explanation of these methods, and how to use them is beyond the scope of this book, but do not worry about this. I will share further thoughts about how you can develop these skills in the concluding chapter, if you so wish.

In a later chapter I will also explain a much easier technique that pretty much everybody can use with little or no training. So, worry not. By the time you have finished this book you will be in a much better position to practice these techniques.

These are very difficult concepts to explain, and are another example of something you either get, or you do not. They are counterintuitive. But as I said, do not worry, every person is different, and processes new information in their own way. Fast is not always better. We still have a few more chapters to explore, and like any good magician I will save the best for last. In the next chapter I am going to explain the importance of 42. Fans of *The Hitchhiker's Guide to the Galaxy* will know all about this, and so soon shall you.

8 THE POWER OF SPIRITUALITY

Do not get put off by the title of this chapter. I am not going to try and convert you to religion or anything else for that matter. What I am going to do is explain the importance of having a reason to live. The number 42 is as good a place to start as any.

Exploring the universe

Fans of *The Hitchhiker's Guide to the Galaxy* will know all about 42, and indeed many books have been written on the subject. All I will say is that it is a number that fascinates mathematicians and is featured in many religions.

In the context of the hitchhiker's guide it is the *"Answer to the Ultimate Question of Life, the Universe, and Everything."*

The meaning of life is a question that has puzzled humans throughout the ages, and I suspect that if I say the answer is 42 it may leave you a bit short on detail.

Spirituality is a subject I approach with caution, and only do so because it is important, and possibly critical, if you wish to raise your performance to a psychoic level. This is a conviction that has slowly crept upon me through my research and work with clients.

My clients usually come to me for one of two reasons. They come to me with an immediate issue that they require help with, or they are long-term clients who are more in maintenance mode, and just wish to keep their performance ticking along at its present, usually very high-level. We get to know each other very well over the months and years and will often start our conversation with what we call a mind, body, and soul check.

Book your annual service

Most of this book has been about the mind, and this is always a good place to start. The human condition appears to have a default state that will take itself back to its previous state over time. That is not what we want to happen when we are trying to cement change, and so we will check a few simple things to be sure that there has been no slippage.

The health of our body is also important for obvious reasons. Our present life is very different to the life that our ancestors led, and not for the better. Like it or not, we have to invest time and money in keeping our body in reasonable shape. We do that for our car, so why should we not take even more care of our body? Having said that I know many people who are not in good shape, and it does not appear to affect their performance. However, these people are the exceptions.

The same comments apply to the soul, also known as spirituality. I have held many conversations with thought leaders in this field, and the consistent message given to me is that it is very difficult to perform at a high-level if one is troubled with spiritual matters, or if there is an absence of spiritual values.

The newspapers are full of examples of apparently successful people who do not appear to live a spiritual life, and yet are hugely wealthy and famous. I hope they are happy too, but in my limited experience many are not. As grandmother said "money cannot buy happiness". I would add that whilst this is true, money can certainly help!

Candles in the wind

So why is spirituality so important? I guess one reason is that so many intelligent and successful people believe it so. Whether they are right or wrong, they regard it as a critical component of their success, and for what it is worth, I agree with them.

George Bernard Shaw may or may not have considered himself a spiritual person, but he knew the importance of having meaning in one's life.

"This is the true joy in life, the being used for a purpose recognised by yourself as a mighty one."

I talk to many people about this subject and am no longer surprised by how many people feel their life is empty, and in extreme cases meaningless. They are not happy, and because of this they will be unable to perform anywhere near their highest potential level. They will not be psychoic. They know there is something missing, but they cannot put their finger on what it might be. Sometimes they ask for my advice. What should they be doing differently?

It is not my job to answer questions like this, nor am I the best person to ask. I suspect that nobody can answer these questions. It has to come from inside the individual. Yet it is a hugely important question and requires some kind of answer. Such an answer includes a consideration of spirituality.

Carl Jung spent many years researching this question too, and his conclusion was that, *"Our main task in life is to discover and fulfil our deep innate potential."* He called this process individuation, and his exhaustive research led him to believe that this is a subject that lies at the heart of all religions. It is *"a journey to meet the self, and at the same time to meet the Divine."*

I am not an expert on theology, but those who are say that religious beliefs and spirituality are in essence the same thing, and that it is possible to be spiritual without practising a religious belief. My experience is that religious or spiritual people usually have a moral compass that can help them navigate life. Life will be full of challenges for all of us, and whilst it is possible to negotiate these obstacles without a compass, it appears to make it much easier if we have one.

Where can I buy a map?

I mentioned earlier that many people feel aimless, and lacking direction in their lives, and ask me for my opinion on how to find meaning. All I usually say is that if the person is in doubt about what they should do, they should follow their passion. How do they spend their discretionary time? Where do they spend their discretionary money? The answers to these questions should produce some clues.

Passion is a much-overused word. When people describe their jobs and careers sooner or later they stress how passionate they are about their work. Sometimes it is obvious that indeed they have a huge amount of passion for what they do. However sometimes it is obvious that they do not. They are not lying, they are just deluding themselves, probably because of what other people think they should believe, or because they are constructing some internal representation of what they think others will respect as an honourable calling.

These people are good people, but they are not authentic, and we can all spot a phoney from 1,000 yards. For such people time spent in deep inward reflection, or with their coach, will be time well spent. There are times when we all need help to identify the difference between what we think we believe in, and what we truly believe in.

If you are in any doubt about the importance of spirituality I will share two inspirational stories of people who faced almost certain death and survived the most appalling physical and mental stresses.

Prisons have walls, but the soul is always free

The first example is known as the Stockdale Paradox. James Stockdale was an American naval commander during the Vietnam war, and held prisoner in appalling conditions for over 7 years. The author James Collins interviewed Stockdale at length whilst writing his book, *Good to Great*.

He asked Stockdale if he could tell the difference between those who were able to survive their dreadful conditions, and those who could not. Who were they?

"Oh, that's easy, the optimists. Oh, they were the ones who said, 'We're going to be out by Christmas.' And Christmas would come, and Christmas would go. Then they'd say, 'We're going to be out by Easter.' And Easter would come, and Easter would go. And then Thanksgiving, and then it would be Christmas again. And they died of a broken heart."

This quotation resonates strongly with me because in the world of self-development 'positive thinking' is a much-overused word, and in my view a fairly useless strategy. A far more helpful interpretation of positivity has come to be known as the Stockdale Paradox, and this is how Stockdale described it.

"This is a very important lesson. You must never confuse faith that you will prevail in the end—which you can never afford to lose—with the discipline to confront the most brutal facts of your current reality, whatever they might be." In other words, avoid the self-delusion trap, but never lose your guiding compass.

I will end this chapter with perhaps the most inspirational book I have read so far. For years many people had encouraged me to read it, and for one reason or another I never got around to it. Until very recently, and I deeply regret the delay, but perhaps I was not ready for it then.

The book is called *Man's Search for Meaning* and was written by Viktor Frankyl. He was an Austrian psychiatrist who survived three years in the concentration camp death camps, and during this time lost his whole family. His survival was a miracle, and the fact that he used these experiences in his later life to establish his psychotherapeutic practice and created the school of logotherapy is even more incredible. This extract from his book expresses his thoughts exponentially more powerfully than I could possibly be able to do.

"Human existence - at least as long as it has not been neurotically distorted - is always directed to something, or someone, other than itself, be it a meaning to fulfil or another human being to encounter lovingly.

For man is originally characterised by his search for meaning rather than his search for himself. The more he forgets himself-giving himself to a cause or another person-the more human he is.

And the more he is immersed and absorbed in something or someone other than himself the more he really becomes himself."

There you have it. Peak performance as part of the psychoic state requires recognising reality from its surrounding delusions, and in harnessing the vast power of the unconscious mind to create the impossible.

The key is to find the sweet spot where mind, body, and soul meet in total harmony. This will be a tough challenge, but the good news is that near enough is usually more than good enough, because we were not designed to be perfect. I doubt we ever will, and nor do we need to be.

Once again there is plenty to think about in this chapter, and some of it is far from pleasant reading. To end on a happier note, I think there is a very good chance you will enjoy the next chapter, and it just might change your life. It has certainly changed mine, and so I will do my best to explain how it has, and why it works. The chapter is about one of my favourite words, synchronicity.

In the meantime, follow your passion, and I doubt you'll go far wrong.

9 THE POWER OF SYNCHRONICITY

In the last chapter I talked about spirituality and how important it will be to us if we wish to be a little more psychoic. I will do my best to explain why and how these two topics could be linked.

Now is the time to bring the big guns out and introduce my favourite psychologist, and his name is Carl Jung. He was a student of Freud until they went their separate ways. Jung was born in Switzerland in 1875 and died in 1961.

As you know by now I talk and write a lot about luck. Until recently I would use the words coincidence, chance, serendipity, and synchronicity randomly as an alternative to the word luck. I am pretty sure that these varieties of luck have occurred to you at least once in your life, and probably a lot more.

An example would be going on holiday to the other side of the world and bumping into a long-lost friend in a shopping mall. It has certainly happened to me on several occasions and I will be interested to know if you have had the same experience?

Our universe is not random

Now I know that synchronicity is far more important than just a word. It is a whole philosophy. Carl Jung was fascinated by meaningful coincidences and described them as synchronicity. In other words, these coincidences were not due to random chance. Jung was not the only person with these views, and Albert Einstein and Wolfgang Pauli in particular were frequent guests at his dinner table. Both of these scientists were Nobel prize winners and took his work seriously, and for this reason if for no other, we should too.

Jung's work is at least as popular now as when he was alive. A synchronicity in my life is that *Synchronicity* is the title of an album by the rock band Police, and Sting is featured on the cover holding one of Jung's many publications in his hands.

When I was a medical student I also worked part-time in the radio and music industry to help pay my bills. Without going into detail, I was asked whether I would consider a junior management job with a group of youngsters who had got together to bash out some music. They gave no hint of the stardom that was to follow.

I turned down the job because I would not have been able to combine it with my medical studies. The band was *Police*, and I just wonder how my life would have changed had I made a different decision. We will never know.

Jung was a prodigious writer and researcher and was also fascinated by the paranormal. He felt that synchronicity could explain the unexplainable. Through his conversations with Einstein and Pauli he was familiar with the concepts of relativity and quantum physics. They all knew, as did others, that these two theories were mutually exclusive. If you believe in one theory the other theory cannot be correct, and this has remained so to the present day. Jung's proposition to square this circle was that synchronicity could be explained as a "falling together in time". Make of this sentence what you will!

I think therefore I am not

Pauli continued to work with Jung, and their over-arching conclusion was that life was not a series of random events, but evidence of a deeper order to life. Jung regarded synchronicity as a spiritual awakening, and part of this deeper order.

From the psychological perspective this concept shifts our thinking away from the over inflated opinions of the ego to the far deeper understandings that surface from spiritual awakening. So, this is a further link to the previous chapter.

Whilst Einstein was far from convinced, he still left his thoughts open to "spooky action at a distance". Interestingly though, he also believed that we do not live in a random universe. He felt that all events are predetermined and these unorthodox beliefs eventually lead to his banishment from his Jewish religion.

We already have enough chapters in this book, but to those of you who are interested to know more about the origin of Einstein's controversial thoughts on this subject you could do worse than research the work of Baruch Spinoza, also known as the prince of philosophers.

Jung's belief that we do not live in a random universe, and his concept of synchronicity, attracted considerable interest, including much criticism. He must have expected this, because although he wrote his paper in 1920 he did not present his findings in public until 1951, and eventually published it in 1952.

Many different paths but the same destination

In the last chapter I mentioned another one of Jung's concepts, individuation. To recap he believed our journey through life has a spiritual purpose, first to know oneself, and then to meet the Divine, whatever that is. A critical component of this journey is that when one begins to understand oneself more fully the ego becomes far less important. When the conscious mind is quiet the far more important unconscious mind has room to speak and to be heard.

Some people call this intuition and I'm sure they are right. I choose to use the word psychoic as an alternative. The word you choose does not matter, but the power that this word conveys certainly does. If you can develop your intuitive skills the payback can be tremendous. You are then far more likely to experience synchronicities, and it is very difficult to explain why this should be so.

This is why I can say with conviction that the next chapter will be the most important so far, and again concerns the work of our friend Carl Jung. The subject is our collective unconscious. The prize on offer can definitely change your life.

The message is pretty simple, although putting it into practice can be far harder. It will be next to impossible unless we can find ways to minimise the effects of our ego and quieten down the frantic activity in our conscious mind. I cannot say that I can do this all of the time, nor can most other people, but I have certainly learned how to do it some of the time. This is more than enough to convince me of its massive importance. I will share my views and suggestions in the final chapter with pleasure.

In the meantime, it might be helpful to summarise where we are at the moment. Throughout the book I have given many different examples of how we can connect to our unconscious mind. The reason why this is important is because the unconscious mind is where we can make the biggest changes to how we think about life, what we can expect from it, and most important of all, harvest the results of our efforts.

You will almost certainly have noticed many new thoughts surfacing whilst reading this book. Some of these thoughts will be very specific, and it will take no great effort on your part to accept them and put them into action.

The other new thoughts may be much less clear and are formless. They are difficult to describe in words because they are vague feelings, and often accompanied with a physiological response. They are feelings that commonly arise from the head, the heart, or the stomach. You will have probably have heard the expression, "I really was in two minds. My head was telling me to do one thing and my heart was telling me to do the opposite."

Sometimes these vague thoughts are even less clear, and an example would be when we get goose bumps, or the hairs on the back of our neck tingle. But one thing is for sure. Wherever, or however, you feel these thoughts, they are going to be hugely important. Because the chances are that this is your intuition speaking directly to you.

When you improve your ability to listen to your body, you will at the same time experience more synchronicities. These synchronicities will be the turbo charged engine that will catapult you and your performance to a far higher level.

The secret of perpetual motion
When you look back at your life, and most of us do not do this often enough, you will recognise that you have already experienced many synchronicities. The difference now is that you can recognise them. Before they were probably all around you, and literally in front of your eyes, but you were blind to them. Now your eyes are open, and you are awakened.

As every chapter passes your psychoic momentum is building. The chances are that the start was slow, and this is not a bad thing. Now the wheel of life should be spinning with a life of its own. No need for will power. Your job is just to watch the wheel go around and round and apply a little lubrication from time to time. Your most important duty is just to the know the wheel is there, 24/7, powering your brain, and everything else too.

I hope the luck is starting to flow for you now, a lot of luck, because the more luck you receive, the more you can share with others, so be generous.

The next chapter describes how we are all connected by our collective unconscious. These ideas will further increase the momentum of your wheel of luck, but there is also a much bigger gift out there for you to grab as well. I am totally serious when I say it can change your life and change the way you think about everything.

10 THE POWER OF THE COLLECTIVE UNCONSCIOUS

I have experienced another synchronicity since writing the last chapter. It was not a pleasant one but it served a valuable purpose and will help me write this chapter. Unusually for me I went to see a doctor last week. I have noticed over the last few months a large mole on my leg. Worse, it is growing, and potentially even worse, it has some black bits in it. I know far too much about skin cancers and melanomas, because I am a doctor, and feared I might have one.

The doctor did not think it was a melanoma but was not sure and nor was I. As expected he recommended an immediate skin biopsy. All went well until later that evening. My over active conscious mind decided to prepare a list for me of all the changes I would need to make in my life when this diagnosis was confirmed. Notice the word 'when', because we already know how our conscious mind likes to invent stuff, and these inventions are usually worst-case scenarios.

Who let the cat out?
Despite my best efforts I remained on tilt until yesterday, though I continued writing. Much to my surprise the anxious feelings disappeared as quickly as they had arisen, even though I did not know the results of the biopsy. And yet I felt I did. It gave me the courage to phone the medical centre, and sure enough the mole was confirmed as harmless.

I am sharing the story with you for a few reasons. The main reason is that this seems to be another example of Schrödinger's cat. When a bit of my skin was lying on a laboratory bench all options were open, and my mind had focused on the worst. At some point a technician prepared a laboratory slide, examined it, made a diagnosis, confirmed this was not a melanoma, and we now knew whether the cat was dead or alive. Happily, the cat is very much alive and kicking!

I know this will appear very fanciful, but I am not making this story up just to prove a point. The formless unknown had become known, even though it was only one technician who knew the result. I knew before I had been told that the result was the best possible one. How did I know? I do not know, but I am certain that it has something to do with the concepts of the collective unconscious, or quantum theory, or perhaps both.

This chapter is likely to be a bit longer than the previous chapters. There are two more stories that I wish to share with you to prepare you for what is to come. I have lifted one from one of my earlier books, called *Get Lucky Now*. If you have enjoyed at least of some of this book I do suggest you read it. There is some useful stuff in there that might help you use more of this new stuff. The other example I reconstructed from a presentation I made last year.

Do not stick to the script

As I mentioned in the introduction, this book starts where *Get Lucky Now* ended. So here is the first story.

"The seeds for this book were planted in January 2014. Like many other people, I always start each year with a cunning plan. My plan for 2014 was to devote more time and energy into presenting self-development workshops. I enjoy the challenge of thinking on my feet and exchanging views with delegates from diverse backgrounds. I get a real kick from watching them as they ignite skills they did not know they possessed. It is fun being a catalyst, not doing very much apart from facilitating them to get out of their own way and find the flow.

My cunning plan turned out to be far from that. Although there have been many other speaking engagements, there have been no workshops, other than a single event in London in January 2014. That is because something very exciting happened there.

I planned to talk about success and how we could learn from successful people to create more success in our lives, too. I never use scripts but instead trust that the right words will surface.

Sometimes this works well while other times it leads to surprises, as it did this time. I asked the delegates if they wanted to be healthier, wealthier, and happier this year. Not surprisingly, they all agreed. Then my brain and mouth disconnected, and I asked a question that was not in the running order.

The question was this: "Do you want to be lucky this year?"

I surprised myself with this question, and the delegates' reaction surprised me even more. A tangible ripple passed through the audience. The delegates leaned forward intently. It was as if time had stopped—no movement, no sound, and my mouth had stopped working, too. I had goose bumps.

I did not understand what had happened, but I knew that one single word, "luck," had just deeply resonated in the reptilian part of everyone's brains. I knew that our single most important desire this year was to be lucky. And I knew that my cunning plan had been replaced with a totally different one.

The new plan was to explore luck and fathom why some people have more of it than others and how we can get lucky now. I spent the next eighteen months researching the enigmatic subject of luck. Had I known how challenging this quest would be, I might not have started. I set some tough goals for myself. They were challenging objective targets in areas that were new to me. The results hugely exceeded my expectations.

I was very lucky, and so were many of my clients. I am going to share some of their lucky secrets so that you can get lucky, too. My goal now is to help you find more luck in your life. You will be the sole judge of whether I used my time productively. I truly hope I did."

I have definitely been on a lucky streak since then. Just believing in luck and believing that we can all attract more luck into our life, becomes in some way a self-fulfilling prophecy, without us having to do too much about it. For sure, I work seven days a week, and this helps. I have done so most of my life, but this time it is different. Most of the work I do now is because I choose to, and I cannot think of anything that I would rather be doing.

This is the other story related to luck. It has proven to be a real tipping point in my life, in the way that I now think about luck, and it did not start very well.

Here are the details......

You will never walk alone

I am taking my mind back to June 2016. I had been invited to a major conference as one of the keynote speakers. This was a great honour and exactly the kind of thing I love to do. I had met many of the delegates before at previous events, and some had become friends over the years. One of them approached me in the morning coffee break. Her name was Sylvia, and she said she had something really powerful that would interest me.

I am always interested in learning something new, but there is a limit to how many new ideas I can take on board at any one time. The subject she wanted me to research was called *Three Principles*, which I had never heard of. I made a note, but frankly did not expect to have the time to take it much further.

In the afternoon I was backstage with my friend Paul McKenna and his wife Kate. I started to feel vaguely unwell but could not put a finger on what was causing my discomfort. I think I mentioned it to Kate. Paul was speaking before me and I told him how much I appreciated having him as my warmup act! I was not disappointed with Paul's response, and we laughed. Both of us knew that Paul is a world-class act, and to put it mildly I had much more to prove than him.

I then sat in the audience and waited for my introduction. As the minutes passed my condition worsened, and I was beginning to seriously wonder whether I could go on stage and deliver the ambitious set I had planned. I tried all the normal breathing exercises but for once they let me down. As a last resort I googled *Three Principles*. I did not have much time, but enough to read a paragraph or two about Carl Jung's related views about our collective unconscious.

Standing on the shoulders of Giants

I knew immediately I had stumbled upon something incredibly valuable when I needed it most. I was due on stage at any moment, and whatever I adopted now had to be simple and fast. I decided that I was going to ride the waves of all those Giants who had gone before me, and who knew a lot more about this stuff than me. I would let them do the talking, and all I had to do was climb on the stage.

And that is exactly what I did. I could hear my voice coming through the speakers on either side of me, but it did not sound like me. I was not even aware that my mouth was moving. I know this sounds somewhat psychotic, but more accurately it is psychoic. Everything I had planned went like clockwork, and others have told me it was my best presentation, and I have little doubt they were right.

Since then I have given much thought to this incident, and it feels as if another piece of the jigsaw of my individuation has slotted into place. However, I do recognise there are still many other jigsaws to complete, so my journey still has a long way to go yet.

My task now is to explain what my research has uncovered and find ways to explain a very complex subject in a way that is readily understandable. Even more important is that it should be relatively easy for you to put into practice. May the force go with us both!

A new era dawns

Carl Jung coined the phrase collective unconscious, and it is probably his greatest contribution to our understanding of how the mind works. It has also been an extremely controversial topic, and in fairness to Jung it is important to remember that his views were first developed in 1916, long before another huge breakthrough in science. This breakthrough was the discovery of the double helix, and for the first time scientists were able to explain the role of DNA in genetics and inheritance. It was pioneering work which gained Watson and Crick the Nobel prize in 1953.

I mentioned in an earlier chapter how a human embryo passes through all stages of human evolution during its embryological development in the womb. With our current knowledge of genetics and DNA it is not such a huge leap of faith to believe that our hard-wired emotions and instincts arise as part of our collective psychic inheritance, as does our anatomy.

Jung believed that our unconscious mind is shared with all other members of our global tribe, living, and even dead. Our unconscious mind is the home of our instincts and populated by primordial images and archetypes. I find archetypes a confusing word, and so take the liberty of suggesting that these are all character traits that have their origins in the reptile brain, as we have already discussed.

The concept of our collective unconscious opens the door to the possibility that our unconscious mind is not only shared with members of our tribe, but with at least some other animal species too, although as far as I know Jung did not propose such a link. If you own a horse or a dog you will likely not be surprised by this statement because there will be times when you feel as if you are talking to each other, or at least sharing the same thoughts.

It does not really matter what we call these deep instinctive desires and emotions. What is important is that we know we have them, know that our lives are affected by them, and affected a lot more than we might believe possible.

As mentioned previously, Carl Jung was a student of Sigmund Freud, until they parted acrimoniously. The main reason for this separation was their differing views on the unconscious. Freud considered our unconscious was personal to each individual, and crowded with sexual fantasies and repressions, whereas Jung considered the unconscious mind as impersonal, universal, and the soul of humanity.

Perhaps their differences were not as huge as they might have believed. Freud certainly believed in some kind of inherited instincts and referred to them as archaic remnants. Whichever model you choose to support, the end result is the same. We like to believe we have freedom of action, but the truth is that many of our behaviours are governed by inherited instincts. Left to its own devices our conscious mind will always try to drag us back to our older and more familiar thought patterns. This is the fundamental philosophy of determinism, a philosophy which is surprisingly shared by none other than Albert Einstein, as I mentioned in the previous chapter about synchronicity.

Talent hot spots
I live in London and one cannot fail to be aware of all the creative genius that has been ignited in this city and continues to be so. Everywhere you go the signs are there. Carl Jung released his thoughts about our collective unconscious during a lecture he

presented at St Bartholomew's hospital in 1936. This is a hospital steeped in history, and not far from where I live. Whenever I walk past I try to imagine myself sitting in that lecture theatre over 80 years ago. How the world has changed since then.

What relevance does the collective unconscious have to our success? My suggestion to you is that it is a critical component in making us lucky and giving us psychoic powers. What do we have to do to use this awesome power? I will answer this question in two different ways.

The first answer is that we have to do nothing. We just have to know that this power is out there for us to tap into whenever we need. It is a timeless source of infinite knowledge and hopefully wisdom. It is like our heart, except our heart does not beat for ever. Our heart keeps beating 70 times a minute, every minute, every month, and throughout our life. We rarely think about it because we do not need to. To do nothing sounds very simple, and indeed it is. The problem is that it can also be the most difficult thing to do, as I will shortly explain.

The second way to answer the question about how to use this awesome power is more complicated, and I am far from sure whether the results will be any different. They might even be worse, because of our common shared failing.

Our failing is that we are human beings, and are instinctively curious, which is good. However, what is not so good is the size of our ego, and our limitless capacity for overthinking. What is even worse is our default state of believing that we can make improvements to anybody and everything that crosses our path.

A common expression is "If it ain't broke, don't fix it." This expression is repeated so many times because it is true, because we keep forgetting this, and I fall into this trap frequently. Therefore, you should approach my following comments with some caution.

I earn my living as a mind coach. People pay for my services because they are stuck in a situation that is frustrating for them, or they desire to move their life to a higher level. My therapeutic approach is to look for solutions to these problems in the unconscious mind, both in mine, and in theirs. I have little interest in the conscious mind, other than its role as the source of many of our problems.

Dream on

I have practised meditation for many years and find this one of the most powerful gateways to my unconscious mind. This is the place where my most valuable creative thoughts take shape, and surface as intuition. The best way I know to liberate intuition in my client is through hypnosis, and it is a lot faster than spending years in meditation.

What do I recommend for you? I cannot give a full answer at the moment, because the next chapter will be devoted to the subject of intuition, and this is where the best answers will be found. For the moment my comments will be brief, and these are two options to consider.

Learn how to meditate. I recommend this without hesitation, and there are many ways to develop the skills. My suggestion is that short and simple will be the sweetest.

Another suggestion is to develop the habit of writing down your dreams. Dreams are also a connection to our unconscious mind, and full of meaning. The problem is that these meanings are abstract and ambiguous. However, there is no question that many unresolved problems can be fixed while we are asleep. It is also no coincidence that this is the one time when our conscious mind is switched off.

On several occasions Jung described his views about the collective unconscious as being the most misunderstood aspect of his work, and I am not surprised. I will share more thoughts with you in the next chapter, and in the conclusion. We are almost the end of this book. I warned this chapter would be a long one, and it could easily have been much longer. At the last minute I ditched a lot of material, and for once followed my own advice that less is more.

I can reassure you that we are almost at the end of our journey. The major remaining subject to consider is intuition. I have already mentioned that I consider it to be our most precious gift and will explain why. I hope the next chapter will be much shorter than this one and will tie together all of the most important ideas that have already surfaced.

I will leave you with a parting comment. I say to all of my clients at some point, "Whatever your problem, I can assure you that you already have the answer inside you. You just may not know where to find it, and it is my job to try and help you to do so."

I have been saying this for at least the last three years, and cannot put my finger on when, or how, this conviction first surfaced. It is only in retrospect that I wonder whether this was yet another intuitive thought that grew in my reptilian brain and originated from the collective unconscious. I will explain more shortly.

11 THE POWER OF INTUITION

I knew from the start of this project how crazy it was to write a book without a plan, or any structure, but fortunately this book somehow developed a life of its own. The Invisible Giants came to my rescue yet again. I knew I would need them, and they did not let me down. Earlier in the book I talked about fear and anxiety, and how anxiety can be the most damaging to performance. Understanding the difference between these two emotions has been instrumental in significantly reducing my stress levels. But not eliminating stress completely. There are times when I wish it could be so, other times when I recognise that without some background stress I may not get much done.

How do I know you will be there when I need you?
The Invisible Giants show up most times when I need them, and then do the heavy lifting for me. But I never know they will be there until the moment. An example is public speaking. This is one of the commonest universal anxieties, and I am not immune to it, and know I am far from alone. What if I knew for sure the Giants would show up on time every time I walked on stage? Then all of my pre-performance anxiety would be removed at a stroke. But it does not work like this, nor for any other performer I have talked to about this subject.

There is a plausible explanation why this should be so. Without a little adrenalin, keeping in mind that a little more than a little is by far too much, a performance would lose its unique edge. It is why live theatre and music is almost always a far richer experience than a studio production. A perfect recording always lacks the magic of spontaneity. Live performance sets the performer free and allows intuition to guide the gift of improvisation.

Improvisation is gift that we all possess, and a little anxiety is the magic ingredient of flow. We may not be able to change anxiety, but we certainly can change the way we think about it. When you have times of anxiety, what difference would it make to your life if you were able to shift your thinking, and recognise anxiety only as excitement? Only you know the answer to this question. All I know is that intuition is one of those Invisible Giants that will help you if you get out of your own way.

I have had to think about this penultimate chapter more than most. At one point I was about to ditch it, at another point I was going to combine it with another chapter, and at yet another point I planned to replace it with the subject of creativity. My conclusion was that creativity and intuition are inextricably linked, yet creativity cannot exist without intuition and so is the best place to start. Great communicators have always known that metaphors and stories are sometimes the only way to attempt to explain complex subjects. I will follow their example. Soccer is the most popular game on the planet and will be my metaphor.

Soccer is not a game of life or death, it is more important than that

For better or for worse Intuition deserves a place in my fantasy football team. Intuition wears the number 11 shirt and is the kind of player that the coach is not sure whether to pick, nor sure what position to ask him or her to play. This player is an enigma and does not appear to do much. Not much running, not much passing, and rarely scores a goal. The player is also not particularly popular with the fans, the Board, or the press.

One of the player's few friends is the coach, who picks him for almost every match, and gets a lot of abuse from the fans in return. The coach survives because he is a good coach and gets results for the team. At the end of the day in soccer that is all that matters.

The secret of the coach's success is that he is psychoic. Because the truth is that when Intuition puts on the number 11 shirt for his team, the team almost always wins. When the coach drops him the team almost always loses.

I agree with the coach. If I had dropped Intuition from this book I may as well have played golf every day during my wonderful stay in Australia. Intuition is tricky to explain, even for the experts, but I think we all know when we have it, and when we don't. Intuition is the glue that sticks all the other things we have talked about together and makes them work. It can make us lucky too.

The power of intuition is recognised by just about every religion and culture, and for good reason, yet they all have the similar problem of not knowing quite what it is, and where it comes from. Here is an example I have used for many years.

I know, but am not sure how

The Zen Buddhist teacher is sitting on the floor in meditation, surrounded by his 11 students. The subject on the agenda today is, you guessed, intuition. In the middle of the group is a bowl containing a single orchid. There is total silence. The minutes pass. The hours pass. Bones and muscles become increasingly painful. Finally, one of the students breaks the silence. In a trembling voice he asks, "What are we supposed to be meditating about?"

The teacher sighs wearily, and replies, "If you ask this question you'll never know."

And that sums up intuition. I mentioned earlier that on the original team sheet I was going to pick one of the established stars for this important game. It was a brave decision to drop Mr. Creativity. He certainly has a great record of proven success. But he is not smart enough to know that he owes just about everything to his team mate, Mr. Intuition, without which there is nothing.

The Oxford English Dictionary of intuition is, "The ability to understand something instinctively, without the need for conscious reasoning."

Can you remember the definitions of psychic and psychoic? I will remind you. A psychic is a person who "appears to have powers of telepathy." This is my definition of the psychoic state and is still work in progress. "The psychoic state of mind is the sweet spot of peak performance that makes people lucky, and lives somewhere deep in our reptile brain, somewhere between the psychotic and psychic states of mind".

One lump please

I could have called the psychoic state of mind intuition, but it is not an exact fit, because whilst the psychic state and intuition are closely related, the psychoic state also incorporates some positive elements of the psychotic state. Such elements include the abstract pictures, sounds, and other sensory bundles of information that are powerful tools to boost creativity. Psychosis is a spectrum, and at the extreme end of the arc is dangerously close to insanity. Psychologist Carl Jung considered schizophrenia to be a result of a close connection to our shared collective unconscious without the smoothing influence of the ego. Suffice it to say at this point that a little sensory psychosis is valuable as part of the creative process, but a little too much is by far too much.

The experts are also baffled by intuition and its origin. Some believe that intuitive thoughts arise from the unconscious mind based on previous experience. Others think that it is an instinct arising from the reptile brain. Carl Jung presumably believed that these thoughts arise from our collective unconscious. It does not matter which model we choose, as long as we know that intuition is there to guide us when we need it most.

I mentioned earlier that just about every culture and religion through the ages has valued intuition. The Hindus also believe that it is knowledge that comes from outside ourselves. Others believe that intuition comes from God, is the source of all creation, a mystical result of spiritual awakening, and the ultimate goal of mankind. I guess this is much the same as Jung's individuation journey to meet the self and the divine. Everybody will have their own position on where and how intuition works. One thing that most if not all people can agree on is that intuition is hugely important.

Intuition formed an important part of Jung's work, and he referred to it as perception via the unconscious. Never one too shy to take his thoughts to the next level he subdivided intuitive people into extroverts and introverts. The extroverts were often entrepreneurs, speculators, and cultural revolutionaries. The introverts were more likely to be mystics, prophets or, dare I say it, cranks. Do you recognise yourself in any of these descriptions?

I guess it must be luck

What we can be sure of is that many people rely heavily on their intuition and are convinced it works for them. They value their hunches. They cannot explain why they are convinced a suspect is carrying a gun, why the price of gold will rise, or the poker player is bluffing, but have learnt to trust their instincts. It can literally save their life. Perhaps it is advanced pattern recognition resulting from years of experience. Who knows, or who cares? If it works for them that is enough.

The unique quality that makes intuition such a priceless gift is that it is a mental processing short cut that bypasses the usual filters and mental processes, and leaps directly from the problem to the solution. It avoids the "What if …?" traps that our conscious mind is fond of creating. There is a time and place for the "What if" questions, but not before the creative process has reached its conclusion. Only then is the time to conduct your risk analysis, evaluate the risk/reward ratio, and be sure that your conclusion was truly intuitive, rather than just wishful thinking.

As you might expect, I talk a lot about intuition with my clients, but surprisingly little about how, and where, to find it. The reason is that I do not need to. If we have taken care of our mind, body, and soul, then intuition will always be working in the background. Just like our heart continues to beat without any conscious effort on our part. As long as we know intuition is there for us it is enough. This thought should bring you great comfort, just as some take comfort from knowing that God or the collective unconscious is always there to draw upon when needed most.

The next chapter will be the Conclusion and I will share some closing comments about the subjects that we have already covered. It will be a review of what I believe to be the most important nuggets and will definitely include further thoughts about intuition. I will also share some final suggestions about how to attract even more luck into your life, should you need it. If you have good luck, you do not need much else.

12 CONCLUSION

I took a long break before writing this final chapter. This was quite deliberate. I needed time for reflection, and to read through the previous chapters again. It took me even longer to go back through the whole book many times and make significant revisions. On the one hand I questioned how it was possible that so many chunks were so poorly written, and yet on the other hand was relieved that most of these chunks contained at least one sentence that was valuable.

The conclusion I reached is that this is the creative process at work. Ideas are generated, often with little direct linkage to the previous ones. Some are useful, many are not, but I recognised that the danger of being judgemental during the early creative process is that it guarantees the flow of creativity will reduce to a trickle.

Another observation is that the book started in a light-hearted way and became more serious as it progressed. I was not aware of it at the time, but it was probably the best approach. I did suspect the book would have its own arc, and so it proved.

I truly hoped that I avoided the temptation to be overly directive. The last thing I wanted was to write a book about "you must do this, you must do that, you must do something else". I was uncomfortably aware that this would be a fine balance and would not be easy to achieve. We are all different. Some people wish only for a few gentle nudges, whilst others want a detailed to-do list. Everybody occupies their own position on this arc. Your greatest friend is your unconscious mind, just as mine is to me. What is certain is that both our minds are very different and will draw very different conclusions based on identical information.

To satisfy as many readers as possible I will draw together the main threads that weave throughout the fabric of this book in two different ways. This is the first summary.

First summary
- Humanoids have walked this planet for at least 10 million years.

- During this time, they were not able to communicate in words, but they were certainly able to communicate in other ways.
- They knew many things intuitively and acted on their instincts.
- They were psychic.
- For 10 million years they survived everything that Nature threw at them.
- They lived in small family groups as hunters and gatherers and may have been happier than we are today.
- Recently, about 50,000 years ago, they did something really stupid.
- They learned how to talk to each other.
- They invented words but were not sure what these words meant.
- This did not stop them using these words to get their own way.
- They lost their psychic powers.
- They became to a degree psychotic, not knowing the difference between fact and fiction.
- Their conscious mind became increasingly important to them.
- They lost the ability to connect to their unconscious mind.
- One inevitable result is they became confused about the difference between fear and anxiety.
- Now we have modern medicine, rarely starve for more than a day or two, and yet the rates of some mental illnesses are higher than ever before in history.
- It is not too late to reverse this trend.
- The common link throughout all these pages is that luck it is not random. We can all make more luck for ourselves, but it will require us to think of the world in a slightly different way. The psychoic way.
- Being psychoic entails finding the sweet spot that unites the psychic and psychotic mind state.
- It is time to be a warrior for The Psychoic Revolution.

You might want to flip through the book another time and make a similar list of what you feel are the key points that resonated with you. Do not worry if you do not know how to use them. Very often these thoughts develop an energy of their own and sooner or later surface as an intuitive light bulb moment.

Second summary

I did suggest that once we reached the end of this book things just might become simpler. The following is as simple as I can make it, and the second summary alternative. Even if you only follow one of these three recommendations your intuition will put at least a bit more luck on your side when you need it most.

There are just three simple suggestions to consider, and here they are.
- Talk less
- Listen more
- Let go of your ego

I will now explain each of these points in a bit more detail. The person you talk to the most is you. This is known as internal dialogue. You will be your best friend if your words and emotions are encouraging, full of appreciation for everything you have, and overflowing with joy. When you allow your inner voice to be critical, whining, and full of doom it will be your worst enemy.

It will take about one month to boost your friend's voice and drown out your enemy's and this is how you will do it. Listen to your inner voice, and every time you hear your enemy whispering in your ear you will politely tell it to go away. You will say to yourself "from this moment forward I will never ever say anything bad about myself, ever again."

In the first month you will have to repeat this mantra to yourself many times. Fortunately, your brain quickly learns how to take any easy path, and you will soon start to notice changes in yourself. Others who are close to you will notice them more. You will not be a different person. You will be the person that you should have been if others had not blocked your natural development.

Your other voice is the one that you use in conversation. You use it not only when talking to friends, family, and in your work but also in your social media, and it can be both in writing or speech form. Be the judge of what is important, and what is not.

The brain power used in conversation cannot be used for anything else, and intuition needs a quiet space to be heard.

The second secret is to listen more to your inner intuitive voice, and this also requires a quiet mind. These are suggestions for you to consider.

Spend more time doing things that you enjoy, where time flies, and when you become increasingly unaware of yourself and of others. Consider taking a course in mindfulness or learn how to meditate. If you are really brave study hypnosis, and in particular find ways to put yourself into an altered hypnotic state of mind.

These options are not as difficult as they might sound. They are not rocket science and you will find it easier than you might believe possible. This is because these are natural skills, innate, and you do not need to invent anything new. You just need to find where these skills have been hiding.

The third and final point is by far the most important, and it is to let go of your ego.

Book a flight into outer space. Anybody who has done so comes back a different person, and often in a spiritual way. Problems that appeared to be so overwhelming on Earth look very different from outer space. The problems are still the same, but time and distance detach them from our emotions.

Only a few people every year have the opportunity to be an astronaut, so for the rest of us the best alternative is to be humble and remember that in evolutionary terms we are just a speck of sand, here today, and gone tomorrow. This thought can be comforting, particularly when you are under pressure. There is also another alternative to signing up for the Mars mission. Remember that as you sleep and dream your spirit is free of earthly constraints.

Remember too that you are not alone in this world, even if it sometimes feels as if you are. You are connected to every other human being through your shared DNA. I have mentioned several times that you still retain the psychic inherited instincts and beliefs from your distant ancestors. Every culture in the world has embraced this concept in some shape or form. To the best of my knowledge it doesn't matter which model of belonging you choose to believe, as long as you believe in one.

Examples of such belonging models include the concept of Invisible Giants universal wisdom, the power of love, God, Carl Jung's views about the collective unconscious, and there are many others to choose from. These are hugely difficult concepts to describe. It is time for another metaphor.

Never before in history have we had so much access to information. Previous generations would consider us to be truly blessed but is this true? Nothing is ever free. Everything comes with a price, a benefit, and a cost. All this information is stored in the Library of the Universe. Even though the information has been digitalised the facility stretches for miles and consists of huge memory banks and is powered by massive computers. Within these data banks is the answer to every question that has ever and will ever be asked. How wonderful.

Unfortunately, if something sounds too good to be true it usually is. The problem with this library is that it is almost impossible to find what you are looking for because there are so many choices. Computer search engines help but you still need to get very lucky to find exactly what you need. The chances are lower than winning the lottery or finding a needle in a haystack.

Fortunately, there just might an answer, and I will repeat the Zen meditation story.

The Zen Buddhist teacher is sitting on the floor in meditation, surrounded by his 11 students. The subject on the agenda today is, you guessed, intuition. In the middle of the group is a bowl containing a single orchid. There is total silence. The minutes pass. The hours pass. Bones and muscles become increasingly painful. Finally, one of the students breaks the silence. In a trembling voice he asks, "What are we supposed to be meditating about?"

The teacher sighs wearily, and replies, "If you ask this question you'll never know."

In other words, the harder you search for an answer the less likely you are to find it. The answer will only come from the previous list of Invisible Giants, universal wisdom, the power of love, God, Carl Jung's views about the collective unconscious, and there are many others to choose from. It will not come *from* you nor should you expect that it will.

It will come *through* you only when you are ready. It will only come at the rate and speed that is appropriate for you, and this will be different for everybody. Slow is as good as fast. The Library of the Universe is a parallel dimension where there is all the time in the world. Just knowing you are connected is enough. Resist the temptation to ask yourself questions such as why and how does this work? You will not find the answer, you do not need to find the answer, you just need to know that this connection works 24/7 in the background, like so many of your other miraculous biological processes.

I have already referred to the inspirational book *Man's Search for Meaning*, written by Viktor Frankyl. I think this extract says much the same thing, but infinitely more powerfully than I can.

"Don't aim at success. The more you aim at it and make it a target, the more you are going to miss it. For success, like happiness, cannot be pursued; it must ensue, and it only does so as the unintended side effect of one's personal dedication to a cause greater than oneself or as the by-product of one's surrender to a person other than oneself. Happiness must happen, and the same holds for success: you have to let it happen by not caring about it. I want you to listen to what your conscience commands you to do and go on to carry it out to the best of your knowledge. Then you will live to see that in the long-run—in the long-run, I say!—success will follow you precisely because you had forgotten to think about it."

This feeling of being connected to something greater than ourselves is both comforting and empowering. It means we have more tools at our disposal than we imagine. This is the way I explain it to my clients, and I keep repeating the message until they get it.

"You already have everything you need to get lucky. You just need to find where it is hiding, and I will help you."

One thing is for sure, this priceless connection to your unconscious mind will be destroyed by overthinking, over-controlling, and by the interference of your ego.

The intuitive thoughts that arise from your unconscious mind can almost always be trusted. Quite simply magic, intuition, and luck are inextricably linked. This is how you will get lucky now.

Are you ready to experiment with these concepts for just one month? If so, you will get lucky. You will deserve to, because you will want to generously share your luck with others. You need more luck. We all need more luck. The world needs more luck. Who knows? We might just make the world a better place to live. That is the true mission of the psychoic warrior.

I hope you have found this book both interesting and helpful. I hope you have found at least one way to connect more closely to your unconscious mind. I hope you have got lucky. As I mentioned, there were many things that I could have written about, but less is more. Once you have digested this book let me know your comments. Write to me through my website www.drstephensimpson.com. You will get a reply, and it will be from me. Advanced training is available for those who are brave enough, so if you are feeling brave write to me. This can be the beginning of our journey together, not the end.

I have also formed a Facebook group, *The Psychoic Revolution*, and you are welcome to join the tribe, and contribute your views. Everybody has a part to play and there are no bosses, because we are all equal.

My final words are these. I hope that you attract a lot more luck into your life. I hope that your unconscious mind will provide the wisdom to use it wisely. I know it will, if you allow it. A common expression in the acting community is "Never give up". It works for us too.

Goodbye for now.

ABOUT THE AUTHOR

Dr. Stephen Simpson is an internationally acclaimed performance coach, hypnotherapist, presenter, bestselling author, and Fellow of the Royal Society of Medicine. As a mind coach Dr. Simpson counts many luminaries from the sporting, gaming, entertainment and business worlds among his clients, including world number one online poker legend Chris Moorman.

Dr. Simpson has appeared on the BBC, ITV, Sky, Voice of America, and other top international TV and radio programmes, as well as in the pages of Sunday People, Glamour, Golfing World, The Best You Magazine, WPT Poker and more, sharing his simple, innovative methods for building luck. As an inspirational speaker Dr. Simpson has delighted audiences of many thousands in Europe, The Americas, Africa, and Asia.

Additionally, Dr. Simpson works as a Mind Coach on both the PGA European Golf and World Poker Tours, helping star performers find their zone, perform in flow, and gain the winning edge. More details of his work, books, videos, podcasts, and audiobooks can be found on his website www.drstephensimpson.com

Aside from this work, Dr. Simpson is passionate about connecting the underserved with quality medical care. During his career, Dr. Simpson has lived in some of the most in-need regions in the world including Angola, Nigeria, Kazakhstan and Oman.

His contributions to corporate international HIV, malaria, and tuberculosis care and prevention programmes are well documented, and have helped millions improve their lives while curbing the spread of this global epidemic. Dr. Simpson was also in Angola with the emergency response team in the fight against Marburg, a devastating esoteric tropical disease and Ebola offshoot. He was also the victim of capture, armed conflict, malaria, dengue, and dysentery.

During this time Dr. Simpson was able to bring his humanitarian initiatives to the forefront, working alongside some of the world's leading change agents, including President Bill

Clinton. He served as a task force member on the World Economic Forum and Global Business Coalition, helping steer the conversation and affect change for millions.

Printed in Dunstable, United Kingdom

64588855R00047